SOCCER BIOGRAPHIES

VINÍCIUS JR.

KENNY ABDO

Fly!
An Imprint of Abdo Zoom
abdobooks.com

abdobooks.com

Printed in the United States of America, North Mankato, Minnesota.
052025
092025

THIS BOOK CONTAINS RECYCLED MATERIALS

Photo Credits: Alamy, AP Images, Getty Images, Shutterstock
Production Contributors: Kenny Abdo, Jennie Forsberg, Grace Hansen
Design Contributors: Candice Keimig, Neil Klinepier, Victoria Bates

Library of Congress Control Number: 2024947818

Publisher's Cataloging-in-Publication Data

Names: Abdo, Kenny, author.
Title: Vinicius Jr. / by Kenny Abdo
Description: Minneapolis, Minnesota : Abdo Zoom, 2026 | Series: Soccer biographies | Includes online resources and index.
Identifiers: ISBN 9781098288884 (lib. bdg.) | ISBN 9781098289584 (ebook) | ISBN 9781098289935 (Read-to-me ebook)
Subjects: LCSH: Júnior, Vinícius, 2000---Juvenile literature. | Soccer players--iography--Juvenile literature. | Professional athletes--Biography--Juvenile literature. | La Liga (Soccer league)--Juvenile literature.
Classification: DDC 796.334092--dc23

TABLE OF CONTENTS

VINÍCIUS JR.

With his lightning speed and unmatched skills, Vinícius Júnior electrifies stadiums worldwide, giving soccer a kick in the right direction!

LaLiga

EARLY YEARS

Vinícius José Paixão de Oliveira Júnior, also known as Vini Jr., was born in 2000 in São Gonçalo, Brazil. He loved soccer from a young age. At six years old, Vini Jr. began playing **Futsal** for a branch of the Flamengo soccer club in Rio de Janeiro.

adidas
CAIXA

Vini's coaches saw his talent and potential. In 2010, he was ready to join the Flamengo youth team.

GOING PRO

In 2017, 16-year-old Vini Jr. made his professional **debut** for Flamengo and quickly became a key player. That same year, he shined in the **South American U-17 Championship**, scoring seven goals to help Brazil win the title!

MRV
TIM
20
TIM
Yes!
VINICIUS JR.

By the end of the 2017 season, Real Madrid announced they had signed Vinícius for more than $47 million! He soared with Flamengo until July 2018.

Vini Jr. moved to Spain in 2018. He soon joined Real Madrid's reserve team, Castilla. And he showcased his skills immediately!

Vini Jr. was quickly moved up to the official Real Madrid team. On March 6, 2019, the winger suffered a season-ending injury.

VINICIUS JR.
28

Vinícius made a powerful comeback and scored his first **UEFA Champions League** goal the next season! His recovery was strong enough to also help Real Madrid secure the 2020 **La Liga** title!

CHAMPIONS LEAGUE
NISSAN
Heineken
PS5
adidas
Emirates

Vini Jr. kept his streak going in 2021. He scored two of three goals to defeat Liverpool in the 2020–21 **UEFA Champions League** Quarterfinal. His performance earned him the UEFA Player of the Match award!

Vini Jr. had a standout 2021–22 season, scoring 17 goals in **La Liga**. Netting the only goal against Liverpool, Vini Jr. handed Real Madrid their 14th **Champions League** title!

WINNERS
UEFA CHAMPIONS LEAGUE 2021/2022

Emirates
FLY BETTER

Vini Jr. started off strong in the 2023–24 season when he scored a goal to help defeat Almería in a **La Liga** match. He ended the season even stronger, becoming the youngest player to score in two **Champions League** finals. He beat out Lionel Messi's record by 13 days.

The 2024–25 season was even brighter for Vini Jr. On December 17, he was named the Best FIFA Men's Player. In January, Real Madrid went up against Red Bull Salzburg. Vini Jr. scored his 100th goal in the game. In February, the forward hit the field wearing the captain's armband for Real Madrid.

LEGACY

In 2021, Vinícius founded the Instituto Vini Jr. to help underprivileged kids in Brazil. He is also on the FIFA anti-racism committee and is a UNESCO Goodwill **Ambassador** for Education for All.

NACIONAL DE LIGA
DIVISIÓN

Vinícius remains a global superstar with Real Madrid, inspiring young soccer players everywhere and proving that dreams can take anyone to great heights with the right kick!

GLOSSARY

ambassador – anyone who is sent as a representative or messenger.

Champions League – a yearly soccer competition organized by the UEFA.

debut – a first appearance.

futsal – a form of soccer played with five players per side on a smaller, typically indoor, field.

La Liga – also known as LALIGA EA SPORTS, the top-tier professional soccer league in Spain.

South American U-17 Championship – a soccer competition held every two years for South American teams consisting of players that are 17 years old or younger.

UEFA – short for Union of European Football Associations.

ONLINE RESOURCES

Booklinks
NONFICTION NETWORK
FREE! ONLINE NONFICTION RESOURCES

To learn more about Vinícius Jr., please visit **abdobooklinks.com** or scan this QR code. These links are routinely monitored and updated to provide the most current information available.

INDEX